i

Copyright

ISBN 978-9914-707-18-2

For permission requests, write to the author at the address below. Ordering Information:

Email: kendik.biz@gmail.com

Social media: @kendikarimi_writes or @kendikarimi

To read more of the author's work, go to www.kendikarimi.com

Cover: Kendi Karimi   *Design & Layout: James*

Chunguli & Kendi Karimi

THE

CAGES

WE

BUILT

A poetry collection by

Kendi Karimi

The freedom of love and the cage of mental struggles

The Cages We Built is a book that openly talks about one's emotional vulnerability and the freedom and right we all have to give and receive love, to be love. But, since this book is written from my personal experiences, it also talks about the things that get us to that point of love. Those ugly scars that make us and the journey of a depressed mind that still leads one to the light. These are the mental cages of life, specifically depression.

Not only is its rate increasing but people are bottling up their emotions with drugs and social media more and more and people need to see that it's okay to openly talk about those 'ugly parts' of us. They still make us the beautiful people we are now who deserve love and whose legacy , at least in part, should be about the freedom brought about from the cages of the mind broken free that once suffocated our human experience.

It's divided into three chapters; freedom, rebellion and the war. Freedom is a section of poems that joyfully celebrate love and intimacy and highlight the madness drunk in the cup of love.

In rebellion, the poems rebel against mistreatment in love and appreciation of oneself as enough as a source of love rebelling against the societal idea of love.

Lastly, the war is composed of difficult poems written during the height of the said depression. They show the clear different mental states of a depressed person when in love and, of a self-loving person when in love. They give more life to the right to experience love in all its flames by showing a contrast of the life lived before and telling the story of that life in rhyme.

That is why, to summarize, the book talks about passion and depression as written on the cover.

Contents

Dear depression,

Thank you for so uninvitedly stomping your way through my yard. Thank you for the mud, the tears and the thuds. Thank you for the snot, the spit and the blood. Thank you for the mess because without it, I would neither have this book nor feel my face warm with happiness again.

After the grass has been stomped on and dried, the only thing it can do is grow again. I sprout dandelions and lilies, yellows and pinks, only because once, I sprouted not. I dedicate this book to you.

See who you have made me become. See how much I love and fall and get back up again. There are seeds waiting to grow on everyone's yard. A little stomping, per usual, is a necessity. Sometimes, a lot.

But remember, the seeds lay there waiting to sprout into hues you never though would color your life.

Ain't what's bad

supposed to eventually

leave you alone?

All along

I've had me

happy me and sad me

Ain't what's good

supposed to eventually

find in you a home?

CHAPTER ONE

Rebellion

There is great power and courage within each and every one of us, even at times when we think we lack it. Once you realize the unstoppable power of self-confidence, there is nothing you cannot achieve.

Even when we are broken, we hope to feel strong at our broken places and sooner or later, after you have embraced your unique self, you become stronger than you ever thought capable of being.

You walk away from self-doubt, from people who bring you down, from negative thoughts and from everything that doesn't bring absolute joy and inner peace in your life. You know what dirty hands look like when they try to grab hold of your light.

You rebel.

Let it hurt

It's in the hurting that we heal

Crash and burn

It's in the burning that you will feel

Kick a ball

Paint only in red and blue

Chop your hair

It's the fighting it that makes it feel like a coup.

//

The one that comes after me

will remind you that I was soft

that I was the poetry you can't forget

the honey you will forever crave

and no matter how much you try

you can never find someone as sweet as me

and thick as mine.

it will remind you I was yours

it will remind her I was yours.

//

The sky was jealous

because of how brightly she shone

dancing to Madonna

And the fellas

were blown

by her flowery aroma

She inspired the ladies

to own their throne

and come out of their hidden corner

Dancing to Madonna -freely-

with her flowery aroma -so busily-

she was able to come out of her hidden corner -easily-

//

I was always enough

you were just never enough for yourself

to take all that I was

I'd had enough

of your miserable self

and your jaws and claws

Sorry not sorry

but I'm done with useless worrying

and the call to your tearing

You're a man who fears caring

and you wanted to take it out on me

so I walked out on you.

//

Allow yourself to experience the stubborn pain in life

so that you will have something to talk about

and something to laugh about

in your old age

with

the

love

of

your

life.

//

I am sorry your apartment still smells like me

I am sorry her face reminds you of mine

I am sorry you can't get over chocolates after me

I am sorry if you kiss her and feel like you're tasting me

I am sorry you can't, won't get over me

Won't drown me, won't bludgeon me

But I am not sorry that I take no bull.

//

You were wrong to think that I could let you back into

my life so easily

after you stomped all over my heart with soiled shoes.

I thought you were the one to wipe your feet off at the

door

I thought you were the one whose intentions were

pure

whose tread was cautious, like that of a deer

so don't expect me to lay out the rug for you now

You're no longer welcome here.

//

Am I difficult? Good.

At least if you make it through

I know you'll have earned the view

and I'm sorry if you can't swim on the deep end of this

sea

my waves were not meant for weary surfers

these waters can drown you so easily

So if you think you need more practice swimming

find another sea to take a practice lap in.

//

I will give you memories

You will remember me

My soul shall not die

In you, I swear I lived.

//

Don't allow yourself

to be bruised so easily

by a person

who can leave you so easily

Don't be so confused

by their blinding poetry

meant to keep you infused

with the aroma of their sorcery.

//

I'm not half a person

searching for my other half

half a heart or half a mind

I am whole, complete

and if not then I aim to be

Before I be with you

I must learn to be with me

completely in my bits and pieces

and once we unite

we will top each other off

like sprinkles on a red velvet cake.

//

Thank you for being my crush

for all this time

I will burn your name in my glass

and let you go. You were never meant to be mine.

I have to let the paper burn out

I have to let all your strength run out

It would have been better if I held your hand

but I accept that things don't always go as planned.

//

Hush

you Ghanaian cocoa girl,

Arabia's gold's got nothing on you

You're a mortal fusion

of earth's brown hues

a melanin goddess

whose skin is flawless.

//

When I say I'm black and proud

I'm not trying to make the white man mad

but there is a little girl out there feeling sad

because there are people out here aiming to make her

feel bad

So don't tell me not to say out loud

that being black should feel profoundly proud.

Don't tell me to hush my sound

when my friend is gunned down,

useless innocence dripping down

still surgical gowns.

Don't tell me to shut my mouth

when the streets are laced with silent screams

of those we now have to grieve

When I say I'm black and proud

put it on a plaque

and pin it in the clouds. //

Have you ever seen a color on skin that's this close to a

chocolate drip?

The very essence of man's molding

is the soil on the ground, which is brown

Genetics don't change

our singular point of origin.

You're a scalding sauna of beauty.

To you who doubt it

the hue of allure

looks very much like you.

//

All I wanted

was a love that loved me

So I sorted

to finding the one for me.

To search I did search

but I never could see

that the love I searched for

was always inside of me.

//

Just like a shooting star

I fell for you

Just like rain on a cloudy day

I cried for you

Just like the sun

I

rose again

knowing that darkness

would soon set in

but still,

I

rose

because your beam

was such a welcoming gift

that my choice of resistance

was taken away from me. //

Pain is part of life

Pain is part of love

You have not truly loved

until you have felt pain

and until you have risen from its ashes

with the hope of falling in love again.

//

Do not be afraid of walking away from love

because not all who you love

have the best intentions for your heart

If it feels like it's too much

or too little

or all at once too ugly to stand

walk away from that trap

Free yourself

from the fear of being by yourself.

//

Silence is only deafening

if there are screams in your head

and a frown traced upon your heart

Love will find you hurt

Love will find all your broken parts

Love will be the glue

that renews faith in you.

//

Do not hold on to a love that brings you more pain

than joy

more rot than growth

just so you can say you have a lover to enjoy.

//

Love is giving crazy a chance

and dancing with madness

hand in hand

Love is romance gone bad

for better or worse

till death do we part

Love is not your first kiss

Love is not the person you missed

Love is.

//

I love how vulnerable I am

how delicately drawn the stretch marks on my skin

act like a map of the amazon of my being

tracing proof that I have lived

I love how often I get to play with my belly

proof of many a nights

spent in good wholesome cheers

sipping beer or porridge or both with friends

proof that I am human

after all

//

Love is not soft kisses under the moonlight

or heartfelt compliments late in the night

Love is not eye flatters and warm hugs

or sunny days and chivalrously quixotic letters in your
bags

Love is capturing but can sometimes do some
scattering

It is wild and at times shattering

It will put the fear of God in you

praying that love never leave you without a clue.

The right kind of love will bring some smiles along

some song and sun to keep you warm

and on some days, soft kisses under the moonlight

and heartfelt compliments late in the night

and you will flatter your eyes

when the one you love hugs you back to life.

You will feel joyous to be in love

when love takes over your whole heart.

//

Do not be afraid to wake up alone

Because alone does not always mean lonely

Don't get a chill in your bones

If you feel so lonely and no one knows

Sometimes in life you will be alone

and other times you will be lonely

at others you will be whole alone

and other times you'll scream out to the world

"Hold me."

//

I know myself

and that's the problem

If I was oblivious to some of my characters

then maybe I would be able to live life blindly

moving forward absentmindedly

but I know myself

Dangerously

And knowing myself is upsetting me

Because I can't seem to change

And be who I want to be

But that also means

I can see it when you try to play me

I'm not as absentminded as I seem to be

Because I know myself

And know me dangerously.

//

How do you define beauty?

Thick thighs?

Snatched waist?

Long legs?

Ocean eyes?

Pouted lips?

Society's concept of beauty is a misconception

an abomination

because beauty is the image

in the mirror,

of the visage

in the mirror

that longs to hold nearer

beauty's cleavage

while bearing it.

Beauty is you as you read this

plain and simple

full stop.

//

I'm like a pineapple;

sweet

but too much pineapple

will leave your tongue scrambled.

I'm a fine apple

tempting

doctor said too many apples

is a damn healthy gamble.

//

Fire burning in my chest

Fire fire lighting up my way

Fire body, fire brain

Chain me down

and I'll breathe fire on your chains.

//

When it's your turn to smile

Make those smiles make a line

Greet them fondly each by each

Smile as much as you need.

//

There's no space left in the world

for women who break other women

Women should water each other's roots

and crown each other with the petals of their flowers

because our spines have ached enough

from generations of abuse over petty stuff

for us to dare cut down

another woman's stem

whether she's up or down.

//

You reflect love

when you love yourself.

Appreciate and spoil yourself

and don't ever feel unloved by yourself.

Even though she is not perfect

respect her

when you make her your main subject.

Inject affection into her needs

correct your expectations

and let time reveal to you what it reveals.

//

Love is its own religion

with the blind faith of a cult

and none can claim otherwise.

It seeks no evil in itself

but to purely conceive

in hopes that you're ready to receive.

It fears not

neither does it judge

its only flaw

is human interpretation.

//

I don't want a lover

nor another best friend

I don't need another

relationship to mend

but if I could, dear friend

not be subtle on request

when summons I, you to me,

to place a kiss on my lips,

do it so devotedly

as a dear friend to me.

_Friends that kiss

//

Yours is not a life to be frustrated

your heart does not belong in a box

it's too beautiful to keep on giving and not receiving.

Your love is beyond any thought

that can ever be conceived by the living.

//

Sometimes you'll be a little much for some people

and that's okay.

A person who is liked by everyone is a good person to
all except himself.

//

Shame on you

for making me feel

like I am less than what I truly am:

a perfectly flawed rebel

with so much life to give

it would suffocate you over and over again.

Shame on you

for making me think

that I have to be reduced to 'smash or pass'

that my physical attributes are what should make or

break me.

The taste of the intelligence in my brain,

would melt every demeaning word from your throat.

Shame on you

for making me believe

that I have to please this and that of you

to be partly accepted.

I accept myself fully

and I hope that someday

you will accept yourself too

because bullies aren't born, they're made

and I can't imagine what made you

but I'm praying for you too.

//

Do not cry at my grave

for I'll be in the air that you breathe

the water that you drink

the food that gives life to thee.

Do not cry at my grave

but if you do

I pray, be brave,

you are only in a temporary place.

Smile

and the sun will shine brighter

Smile

and the crops will grow wilder

Laugh

and your days shall be longer.

Do not cry at my grave

when my bones lay rotting below

I'd hate to see you so enslaved

and worse, so very low

(you know I'll see you again).

//

Do not boast, dear death

for death shall die before I do

If you don't believe

the words I say

then watch me live

till my praise days

for death shall indeed take my body

but from eternity

my soul it cannot grasp.

therefore

death shall die before I do

and there's not much about it

that death can do.

//

Don't be told

you're too wild

to be tamed like a flower

you are the flower

a wild flower

enchantingly wild

Don't be told

you're too old

to be fully devoured

Only a coward

would hurt you like that.

//

Worshippers of the invisible God

are mentally framed and quite conceded.

As it were, they only see within the lines

that were long ago, as believed, kneaded.

As it were, they only see within the lines,

to live with lust prohibited in their book,

singing, drinking Jin all day, all until Sunday

where they bow their heads, repentful a look.

Singing, drinking Jin all day, all until Sunday

is what dooms the fate of these worshippers.

Their judgment day creeps in,

jin will be the least sin when sinners scream, "Help us."

Watch me still worshipping an invisible God

and drinking gin all day, even on Sundays,

and trying my best to live a life without hate

for love is the only key that opens heaven's gates.

//

I'd rather be an atheist

than be a believer

who action upon action

is doomed, salt on wound,

jinxed

But I am a believer

who believes in love

and if love itself wrote the spiritual texts

maybe I would believe in them

but I believe in The One God, and that's that.

//

I wish I could touch, not the stars

but the bright streak that flash by

I wish I could taste, day in day out,

dawn and her brother dusk.

I wish I could be a cancer cell

so that I would gather my troops

and together in unison

set ourselves ablaze and finally die.

I wish half of my body

could be dark as the space in a closed box

and the other half

could be whiter than the fluffy clouds

and following suit, seven billion heads,

that way; one plus one would equal to one.

I wish I had the mighty power

to control the hand of the God of Muhammad and the

father of Jesus

that way I would fuse them together,

melting one in the other

as a blacksmith molds his sword, creating a nation of

brothers

and mortals, upon witnessing this with their eyes,

would celebrate together,

laugh together

and even share a meal,

all worries and bias aside.

I see, I see,

I can be none of these

I can do none of these

but if I could

oh if I could

I reckon I'd also let things be

because things are clearer seen,

more felt and better understood,

when they are naturally experienced

or experienced naturally.

I reckon life with its seven heads

can still bow down those heads

inhaling from source, exhaling back to source.

I reckon life can be this peaceful

even as we die or feel like we're dying everyday.

//

.

So many of us women are lost

in so many lost boys acting like men

boys who do not know themselves well enough

to know us deep enough

boys who hide behind compliments

to cloak the impotence of their pursuit

when met with a woman with a bigger income.

You too are trapped in fear my dear,

of fighting against the hardships you would have to
face,

if you decided to fund your wallet by yourself.

One person wants money,

the other wants sex,

both have lust and ego, what next?

Awareness. //

Drink yourself up darling

you deserve a little more you each day.

//

Teach them how to love themselves and they will love

you back in return.

Go hard for them when they need you most and they'll

go harder for you when you can't.

Teach your sons and daughters about art

So they may be curious about life's so many parts.

//

If he loved you

you wouldn't be bent like a question mark in defense

wondering, "what next?"

If he wanted you

you wouldn't be twisting your neck

trying to catch a speck of his attention.

//

It's not your fault

you are not to blame

you are more than enough

they were just never enough for themselves

to appreciate your tornado self.

they ate in pinches

you ate in handfuls

they drank wine from a glass

you downed the bottle in an hour and a half

they were sand

you were grass

it's not your fault

the relationship stopped

you're not to blame

for both your pain

you're more than enough

I hope to God you can see that.//

Boys get sad too

they've just been taught

that sadness is not an emotion

a man should feel

-or if he feels it, then he should not show it

but he does feel it

even when he's trying so hard not to show it-

that strength is a man's greatest quality

that they should carry their problems only in their
heads,

because it's their responsibility to be 'the man' and act
like it,

that should not be the case.

Allow yourself to feel exactly what you need to feel,
how and when you need to feel it.

//

I don't want perfect

perfect has not lived

perfect will refuse to live freely

perfect will be too perfect for me

I want flawed

a sort of thunder

a sort of hailstorm

a fall of snow in may

a blessing disguised as a mistake

just like me.

//

You don't have to be mean to be selfish

Self-love is a justifiably selfish and rebellious act

one meant to wipe the blemish

of the side-tracked fact that other's love comes first

The world has taken too much from us

for us not to deserve a galaxy of love and beyond

from the galaxy in the confine of our own hearts.

Self-love is a one-ticket bus

to a place better than earth

a place where me and I are sweethearts.

//

Be one with yourself

selfish with your heart

and generous with your love

and let that love plant deep roots in you first

and let it yield fruit

and let your inner intangible

taste buds meet

with the juice of this fruit

the pulp

the sweet.

Be one with your self

and you will be yourself.

//

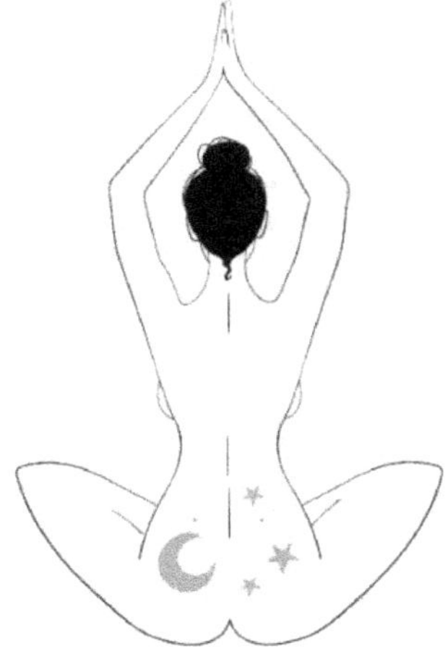

You are reaching for the light that is rightfully yours

Your eyes are so bright when you think you've met Mr.
Right

but Mr. Right doesn't treat you right.

You're a chore, you're sore; more, more, more,

He's your only cure

to the poison he delivers.

//

Why are you seeking

revenge on your body,

when you should be seeking

a revenge body?

//

I opted for a paper and pen.

I opted to take a deep breath.

The sirens were loud in my head.

I opted for a prayer instead,

Instead of calling shotgun

In death's car, before my life has even begun.

//

Maybe if time could go back

things would be different now

but maybe is just another could have,

would have, probably should have

but eventually never was.

So why dwell

trying to swim

in a well

I can't see?

//

You cannot rise before you fall

Fall

You will rise.

Potency is derived from a range of emotional

vulnerabilities.

You can't say you know how to get over something

if you have not experienced it.

Emotional exposure is holding yourself accountable to

the growth of your soul

which in turn grows your whole

You cannot rise before you fall

Fall

You will rise.

//

Allow yourself to feel

not just the love

but also the pain

for the pain will build you up

so much stronger

and give you the shape

of a love

so provokingly serene

to your being

it will make you much wiser

and only a few will dare venture

because the time wasters would see danger

of the karma of the avenger

they would see maturity in your eyes

and they will fear playing with that.

Only the deserving

will try to deserve you.

because you deserve

someone who deserves you.

//

Oh, but darling

didn't you know you can fly?

Just because he plucked a few feathers out

doesn't mean that new feathers won't sprout

and even if new feathers do not grow

who is to say

that the ones you have left

could not soar up high

and teach the very same men who broke you how to

fly?

Who says that just one feather,

cannot sign off on a war so big,

cannot bring apart all that was once together?

Just one feather

can have power like this.

Now consider the power of a human being

who controls this feather; *his will.* //

Sell yourself short, and they will always be bargaining

for the cheapest price.

Show them they need to up their game to afford your

time,

and you will waste very little of your time,

but more importantly,

you will find people who will make you a priority

not some minority in their fantasy.

People who will not love you reluctantly

but with fearless urgency.

//

What hurts your soul the most

is that you refuse to let go

of everything that once disguised itself as a charm of

affection.

You refuse to burn those old clothes

with oak scents,

and instead, choose to repair them,

by sewing them back up

and the needle pricks at your skin

with every stitch,

but you insist you will be fine,

that the clothes, once worn,

will look brand new again,

but darling,

the days they have seen,

could put a million soldiers to tears,

a single cloth wiping the tears of a million soldiers for

years.

Set down the burden of faking happiness

be upset and relish the madness.

Charades fade, say it with me, "charades fade."

Don't blow your heart with that grenade.

//

We search for love in other people's hearts

trust in other people's character

hope in other people's spirit

while really, we just have to awaken to ourselves

and the rest will take care of itself.

//

One day

It won't hurt anymore.

One day

You will be okay

and one day

you will smile.

You will love and be loved

and you will realize

that all your pieces

once broken

never really were

and that you were strong enough then

even without knowing it

and you are stronger now

as you realize it

and now that you know your strength

the upsurge of its might can't be overturned

It might not be at this moment

but your STRENGTH will surge

sure as waves in the ocean do surge.

//

Come in with your scars

let me treat your wounds

tell me the stories

that made you, you.

Love me enough to be naked with your pain

and trust that i will jacket it inside my chest

and so preciously hold it close to my breast,

forever,

and then, I will stretch out this forever even longer,

and cover it within the jacket of my being

because where I am you are with me

and God himself can see this.

//

You can't expect someone to love you if you do not know how to love yourself first. That's something that I've come to learn a little late in my life, and it's left me with scars that will fade in time but a heart that is stronger than I ever would have imagined. It's part of the process of life where you off put something by releasing excessive desire in contrast to its original home.

At least now I know that being by myself is not the worst thing after all and I neither search for nor cling on to the approval of other people, nor act based on their possible judgement.

If someone doesn't like what I have to offer, let them go buy in another shop.

You have to be brutally honest with yourself if you ever want to make progress in life. It took me a while, but once I did, it ripped me a new map to how I see and feel things. I accepted the change because change is inevitable and, it's the best part of this whole adventure. I changed and this new me is patient with feelings because she once felt them in the sense of a comfortable desolate place. All along it was a garden!

To *you* who once made me feel so so small:

Ulikuwa ready for war, ati ulikuwa sure

I can't defend myself because I'm poor

but Mimi I was built for war

since niwe msmall hadi nikamature.

Home ndio watu huita war zone

and its what's built my bones

hadi nikakuwa yule bazu

na kurun from home

haiwezi fix my inner holes

but if you come for that throne

I'll come for your bones

na hiyo uneza kuwa sure.

I can defend myself, and I'm not poor

I've got a bank inside myself

hio home ni true kuliko hio mapua.

You were ready for war, apparently you were so sure

I can't defend myself because I'm poor

but darling I was built for war

since I was small until I was mature.

Home is the place people call a war zone

and its what's built my bones

until I became a bone whore

and running away from home

can't fix my soul

but if you come for that throne

I'll come for your bones

and that, you can be sure.

I can defend myself, and I'm not poor

I've got a bank inside myself

and that home is truer than that nose of yours.

//

CHAPTER TWO

Freedom

The energy you emit into the world will always come back to you. If you are always negative, then negative things will always be happening to you which will make you more negative and the circle of negativity will continue.

Change the way you think about yourself, and how you perceive the things that happen around you for good, and you will change your life for the better.

You have suffered enough, you have fought the war, you have learnt how to rebel and now it's your time to enjoy the fruits of your labor.

It's your time to enjoy every single bit of love and appreciation that comes your way as a result of letting go of negative energy because you deserve it. Infinite love awaits your thirsty heart, so so ready to make you fat.

Don't be shy. You are free. Drown in your freedom. This love is yours to eat (too).

Look at the way she moves

Does she not resemble the gods?

Don't her crown glow divine?

Bittersweet sadness, depression improves.

Look at you

falling

at

odds

with the moping you thought would be forever yours.

//

It is not my promise to love you

nor my aim to choose

between you and the world

but if a choice was presented

I'll tell you this,

but first come for a kiss

come kiss these lips waiting for your lips

walk right in

to my destiny

and build with me a space ship.

Let's find land where no one has been

and impregnate love in that space free of jealousy.

//

"And when you leave

What will be left of me?"

Her voice was low, her face drooped.

"Leaving was never an option."

"But you will and so will I. We shall die; me before you

or you before me. What will happen then?"

Then, I would get to say that my life was complete

because we lived and we loved.

We had this, we had **IT!**

And this can never be had by anyone else but us.

I will knit myself a sweater with grief

with threads made out of your memories

and every tear of yours that I will miss to kiss

will be swooshing inside my heart like water carrying a

leaf.

Then, you and me might be history;

the mystery of history is its slippery slope

but then I'll fall and fall with some hope

knowing the end of my rope leads to you.

To me, that is victory.

//

91

You want me to be honest?

I don't want to go to work today

I don't want to move a step out of bed

I want to stay here

and sweat it out with you

and get so absorbed into your skin

like a fish growing a new fin.

Whose lips are these?

Whose hair and sweat is this?

What is whose and where does it begin?

I want to place my ear on your chest

and listen as your heart dances

and you will say to me something like,

"listen to how wildly it beats because of you..."

and I will press my breasts against your chest

like mud romancing fallen branches.

your presence is dreamlike

and I want all the droplets of your dew

and when we lose our jobs

we will laugh about it

for what are the odds they'd let me put a bed by my

desk, watch me lay with you and permit it?

//

She tasted of adventure and fresh mint

of autumn leaves and blooming flowers during spring

he wanted to run wild along her road

meet her sea and swim deep in it

he wanted to taste her spirit

and drown in her soul.

//

The world was falling apart around me

but here I was; eating chicken

with a view to die for

Atticus in my hand

God in my heart

him on my body.

The world was crying blood and screaming war

and I was not so torn

between where I should go or,

with whom I should sleep beside.

I can forego art, I'll go for your heart.

The world was falling apart around me

the world was crying blood and screaming war

and I was exactly where I needed to be

with the core of my whole whom I much adore. //

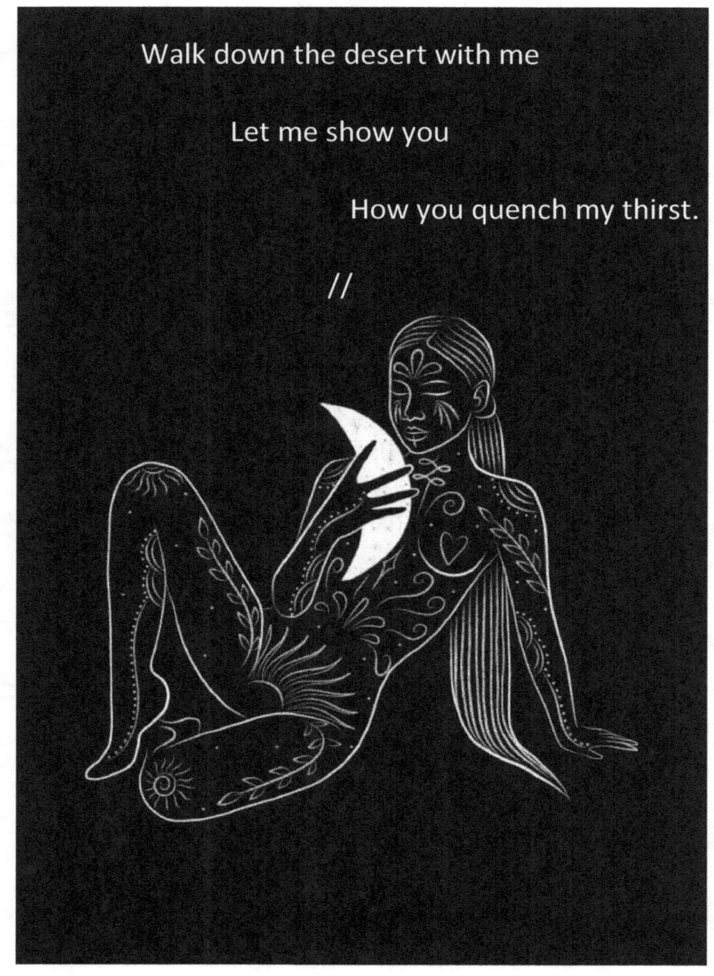

Walk down the desert with me

Let me show you

How you quench my thirst.

//

I want to inject myself with your love

and feel it pump in my veins

I want my heart the size of a dove

so you can eat it like you have my brains.

You want? I'm here

Come tell me ear to ear

Come tell me if my brains

are not woven by your love's veins.

//

There will always be a paper flying in the wind

a river dancing down the stream

a bird hatching an egg...

There will always be the words you say

and those that you keep within

There will always be the feelings that you evoke in me

there will always be the memories we make

the songs in our wake

the cries, laughter and smiles we create

There will always be a heart that beats for you

continuously shattering

D-dum d-dum d-dum d-dum

for you.

//

Learn to get lost in the lovers religion

no book or iPhone can teach you that

learn to be like the pigeon

fat with commitment to who holds your heart

once you get a sip of this type of love

don't stop being a drunk

choke if you have to, choke and rest, but don't stop

don't close-up shop

when love seems like it's lost

and your windows sit closed .

Maybe that is why love seems like it's lost.

//

He has a presence

that lurks in the shadows of my happiness

I pray he keeps my heart safe.

He has an essence

that scrapes off my sadness

my heart's locked in his heart's safe .

//

There are

treasures

hidden

between

her legs

and she

has given

you the

map to find

X.

//

Her tongue was soft

but her laughter was softer

It is not her physical attributes that knocked you down

-albeit as marvelous as they were-

it was her way of being:

the water waves behind her voice

the infectious synergy around her

It was everything that made her her,

that spiked your chemical reactions

and it was the way she decided to love herself

that left you feeling bereft of love

Her tongue was soft

but her heart was softer

you left thinking it would grow hard

but all it did was glow the flowers in all her parts

she was soft and she was loved by her

and she doesn't regret what you were

but she wanted a man who would stick around

every time there was a new her to be found.

There was no version of you like that

and that fact was sealed like that

because love is important

and just as important is self-love.

//

The devil winked at me

with your heart held in his hand

(Too good to be true)

but I made a run for your heart

There was no price to pay

for nothing would ever be

as valuable as that which he held.

Stunned, he said, "That wasn't very wise."

I replied

"You've never looked in to his eyes."

"I have," he said, and I called him a liar.

The devil winked at me

with your heart held in my hand

too good to be true

I made a run for it.

//

It was such a beautiful night that day

and all I wanted to do was stare at YOU

Forget the stars that shone

forget the moon, forget the phone

forget the angels in my head

repeating the words you had just said

YOU

YOU

YOU

ME

ME

ME

US

WE

That's all that mattered to we lovers to be

//

She was the closest thing to God that ever

walked the earth

And I was lucky enough to worship at

her feet.

//

I could die without love

I could die without hate

But

I would rather die with a cup full of bitterness

and have tasted a sip of your love's eagerness.

//

Read me like a book

flip the pages between my legs

gently

Lick your fingers and flip…flip…flip

this is how you make poetry out of me

Lick your fingers and dip…dip…dip

this is how you make music out of me.

//

Tight jeans and a summer smile and I was hooked

Brown eyes looking at me and I was cooked

Damn it! My heart was already booked

but tight jeans just looked and looked and looked

and just like that, the spark was overcooked.

//

You're a little less human

a little more God like

The touch of your lips

and the graze of your fingertips

leaves butterfly tremors on my hips.

My skin electrifies in anticipation

tasting a hurricane of emotion

from your parted lips.

Your touch is a sensation

I don't ever want to miss.

//

I'd rather fall a hundred times

and bruise myself fatally each time

than never fall for you at all

so I'm keeping my body tight

and my aura high

cross my heart and hope to die

that our chakras intertwine.

//

Before he touched my lips

he first kissed my mind

and that is how I died.

It is not his hands that undress me

it's the vibrato in his voice

the undoing of all mankind.

//

Paint me on an empty canvas

I'll strike a pose for you

or stroke the brush against my skin

whichever way will do.

//

Tough luck, says life

hold my hand, says love

I'd be lying if I said

you make my knees weak

The basic functioning of my legs

acts as if it's completely diseased

I'd be lying if I said

I ever thought of us like this

of me so love-infused and open

of a version of me that isn't so very broken.

//

He was the deadliest sin I had ever made

the risk that made me so unafraid

and I would be lucky to fall from grace once again

and walk away from the sun to the heavy rain.

//

Kiss me in places that make me tremble

I'll take care of my lips

you handle the rest

Assemble me as I crumble

and slip into bliss.

Ensure you're firmly pressed

against my hips

You are much more than I expected, Mt. Everest.

//

He smells like a mix

of spring and rainy days

On hazy days

lets have lazy days

In crazy ways

lets love

and never change.

//

Hold me at my sensitive places

legs

wrist

waist

Taste the galaxies that you turn to dust

when you make my stars explode

carry me along the milky way of your face

let me graze

each bump and edge

legs

wrist

waist

Don't stop the rhythm

Don't slow the pace.

//

The features of your face are like a prison cage:

brows thicker than bars of steel

eyes deeper than a keyhole, they make you feel

and my body can never escape your cage

I'm shackled to you till I age

like cuffs to a wrist in the heat of bondage.

//

Study my body like a map

discover the Niagara falls

climb to the top of Mt.kilmanjaro

taste the salty waters of the Atlantic

and when you're ready

find your way to the crown jewel

where your home lies.

//

This is how we make music:

like your mouth has the gift of singing

and I am your favorite song

verse by verse

in this hymn of ours

we're immersed

in singing for hours

Every note accelerates the pulse in our bodies

We're fully submerged in the making of art.

//

I pray you don't treat my heart like a pile of rags

because every time I am in your presence

I feel like I am on drugs:

my head spins

my heart aches

my palms wet

my pits sweat

and I'm met by je ne sais quoi at the gate of my heart

knocking, smiling, tempting a tempting start

My tears are blowing in the wind

because of how pleasant you've made everything

seem.

and you know what?

if I get to feel like this everyday without a fault

tip-toeing on the verge of the sea

and you right there with me,

I will be the happiest and luckiest fool that ever was, is

and shall forever be. //

I call to you

like rain to thunder

You answer obediently

with zero decency

Be both gentle and rough with me

Envelop me in the sweetest ecstasy

Sweat with me skin to feeling

feeling everything outside like we feel within

You saliva smearing machine

rotating with the kinetic energy of a turbine

we're leaving tracks of lost innocence

behind the climax of our sighs genesis

I'm open to it

If you'll teach it to me

I want to be so skin to skin to feeling with thee.

//

There is a god between her thighs

and you worship there every day

You don't forget to give to the full moon

an offering for what it has given to you;

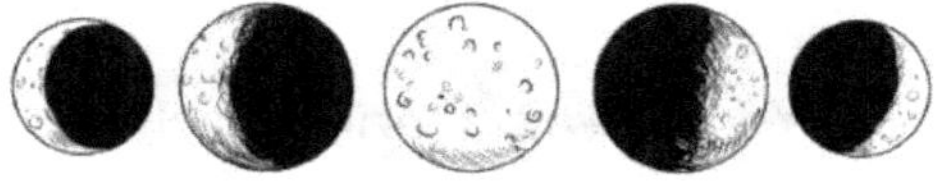

enough light to see her even at night.

//

126

You are so beautiful inside

because you see beauty

even where beauty doesn't reside.

Your outside is beautiful too

but I'd degrade you

if I defined you by such vain and common lenses

Your intelligence is your beauty

your grace more fair

I wouldn't know what to do

if I hadn't fallen in love with you.

//

Eyes so infinitely defined

you'd think they were divine

I wouldn't be surprised

if you broke out in to light

Only a person touched by the heavens

would radiate the glow that is in you

and I don't care to rhyme

as long as I die, die with you.

//

I has never seen dapperness

as impressive as yours

call me a rend, fool or the like

but I shall spend time with tools like the bike

to cycle the earth round and round

and preach of the love that I have found

as long as you're with me on the rounds.

//

You are the beginning and the end

and all that begins ends with you

The pot of my bubbling heart

is covered by your hearts lid

there's a sizzle in our broth

when each to each we become both

I was just a wandering fool

who wondered right to you

and as I boiled my heart to mist

I knew my end was just beginning.

//

Let your heart live with love

and you will be young forever

See how hate breaks your heart

see the damage internally done

let your heart live with love.

//

If you think Eucharist is divine

then you haven't savored your lips like I.

If you think the church is heavenly

then you haven't appreciated your presence.

If a nation is blessed and blessed

then you my dear are the cause for its salvation.

//

Even a rose grows from dirt

so accept my frail heart

and let us bloom

through the thorns and petals

stinks and scents

and

hopefully

in spring or summer

we may attract a bee or two

or ten.

//

Take me away

carry me

like leaves are carried

on a windy day.

Dance with me

like the ocean breeze

dances with the bubbles in the sea.

Allow me space

to hide my face

in your heart.

//

Let's not tell of our love

Let's keep it in our hearts.

No other ears need to hear

No other eyes need to see

but if they do hear and see,

like a phoenix, we will rise

from the stares of wicked glares

for our love is like

the trepidation of spheres.

//

I don't deserve to hold your face

I am unworthy of your beautiful grace

You wiped the windows of my soul clean

and imped my feathers in your wings

Mistakes I've made in great a span

and I didn't think I deserved you

with all that I'd done

but you showed me broken things

are worth as much as beautifully woven things.

//

He doesn't ask if I'm okay

He knows when I'm not

He wraps his arms around me

and waters my garden.

My flowers grow

because of him

They do not wilt

they do not wither

for he is always gardening

removing any weeds

that dare root themselves in me

He plants hundreds of little seeds

that bloom into striking flowers

sometimes trees grow

and during autumn

he picks up his rake

and tidies me up pretty neat,
and when spring comes along,
I share my fruits with him
for he has warmed me during summer and winter too.

The cycle continues
autumn, winter, summer, spring
and still,
my gardener never tires
to cultivate the garden in me.
//

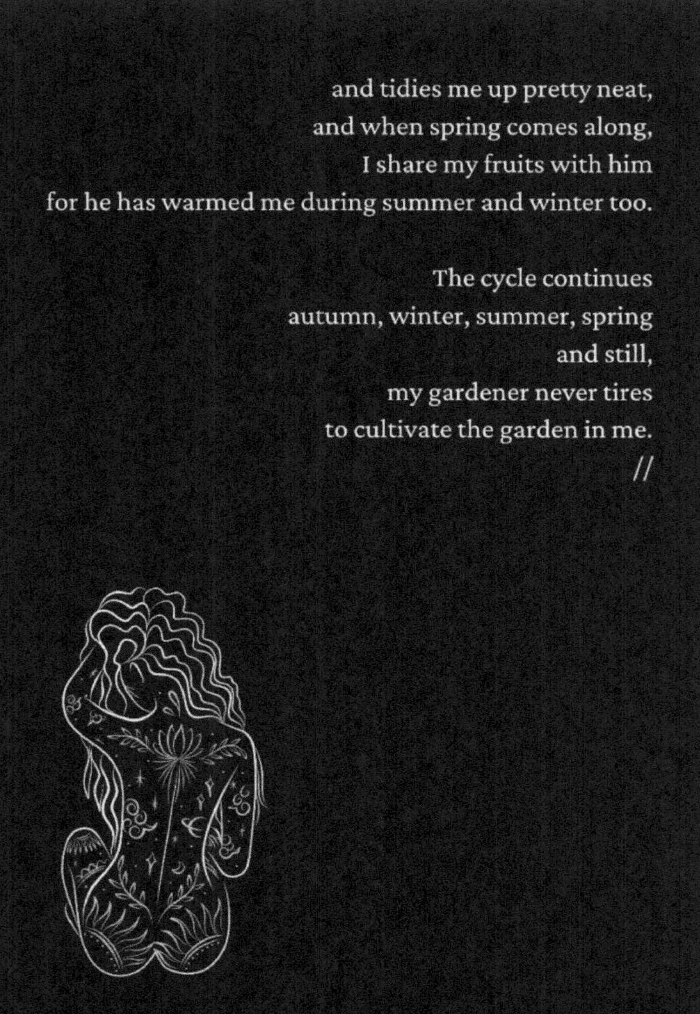

I am fish

I live in the sky

I am alive

and breathe in your smile

I am fish

I need no water

I need no air

You just keep smiling.

//

How long will I love you?

Till the end of the world?

But the world is always ending!

From dawn to dawn?

What if the world ends today at noon?

Till man's extinction?

But we'll all be dead!

Maybe when the sun dies,

then love will die too?

I have questions I can't get answers to

All I can do is love you.

//

It's okay

You take my breath away

Don't be shy about the way you make me pray for

better days

It's okay

Exhale the resistance away

Don't run the track and refuse to meet me half way

It's okay

You're okay

We'll be okay.

//

I stand cold and naked before
you
and await your ugly scorn
but you hold my palm to your
pounding heart
as a mother to its newborn.

I'm demure with my body
and my skin is as soft
as a child a new
skin that's gently melted by
you,
a skill mastered by few.

My diamond mine melts and glows

and aches for the miners' pickaxe

a drill that twists my aching parts

as you love me deaf, blind and now!

Still, my hips burn with shyness

and my face meets my palms

but your lips touch my warm cheek

as we swim deeper in the dams.

//

Heaven has brought me a disease

your movements are no stranger to this

now I'm hooked on you and I'll need my fix

I'll need my body to regularly tremble with bliss.

Thank you for giving this girl

a woman's needs

I have genuinely tasted lust

but, could this also be love?

I guess I'm a girl

so I had to ask that.

//

Kiss me like you're mad

Dare to catch my heart

Dare to dream

and start.

//

I was the wilting flower, and you were the water that

drizzled me back to life.

I was a coward, but when your flower needed care by

the hour,

I used some of the water you sprinkled in me

to water your roots

with water to breathe

That is what love is.

//

He said he wanted my heart

I asked him what piece

he answered all of them

One by one

to the thousands, he would bend his back and gather

I told him thousands was a fraction

of the chain reaction of a broken heart's actions

I told him some pieces were heavier than others

some much darker

yet still

day after day

he kept on collecting the fragments

one by one

piecing them back together

into something that looks like a heart

he made my whole lighter

Making my heart brighter

he taught me the punches of a fighter

and the gentleness of being a farmer

overall, the chain reaction of a broken heart's actions

still led me to my heart's companion.

//

*I want to trap divinity in canvas
and paint you like I'm searching for God and his answers*

I took portraits of you in your sleep

as you awoke

in the shower

Maybe today

you will learn to love that scar

in the fading polaroids

that I will keep on taking

and if not

I hope you will let me

kiss that scar I love

I will never tire

trying to show you

just how beautiful you are

even with your beautiful scar.

//

I just want to know

why God didn't wake up my spirit

so I could watch him create you

Radiant doesn't cut it

nothing could, nothing would,

nothing ever will.

I just want to know which alley I was lost in

when God was dishing out

a blessing such as you.

//

You are not a catch

you are not a ten

because no one could ever catch you

nor quantify you

The goodwill of your heart is a thousand light-years

away from infinity

so far inside the good heart of God's patience with the

human race

that's why fear has me subdued

if you let me love you,

there's no way I can get over you.

I admire you like a forbidden fruit.

//

CHAPTER THREE

The War

In life, there often comes a time when one experiences a dramatic ejaculation of depression. Be it great sadness that overwhelms or a cup that runneth over with emptiness, and more often than not, man's body or spirit is either broken or severely weakened by the trials of human life.

This is a daily struggle for most; the moments of self-doubt and the darkness that builds a home in some. The tears that water the earth. The yes that should have been a no and vice versa. The maybes stuck in your head that should be long ignored.

This is the war.

Ps: the war is a difficult section, but a necessary one. From it, you will understand where the right to freedom and rebellion have flapped their wings from.

Lonely.

Lonely was

Lonely and

Lonely wanted me to sprout a new branch of feeling.

Lonely did not want to always feel so

Lonely. But lonely was so

Lonely. Hold me,

Lonely said and I held

Lonely. Hold me,

Lonely said again, but I had already held

Lonely. Hold me, hold me...

Lonely I'm here, hold me. But

Lonely could not hear me.

Lonely was blackout

Lonely and

Lonely wanted to know me. Do I let

Lonely in? Do I let

Lonely in? Oh -

Lonely couldn't hold me, because

Lonely screamed hold me from inside cold me. Oh -

Lonely, you do know me.

Lonely tried to hold me. I talked to

Lonely a few minutes ago.

Lonely reminded me how

Lonely it feels to be so

Lonely.

//

She felt forgotten

and so she left

and in her leaving

she was remembered forever.

Her mind felt rotten

her heart always exposed to theft

she lived in constant beating

by the club of her behavior .

I'm trying not to think

as I slip into dreams

I'm trying not to sink

into my self-defeating whims.

I'm trying not to be

such an alcoholic

trying desperately to see

life in all its magic

I'm trying.

//

You said my skin felt like the melting of a candle

all fired up to the touch.

It felt like a bundle

of pain a bit much.

You could feel the hailstorms of my rage

shattering the love that you were bringing

and I couldn't find a safe space to place my rage in

so you let me win

because you couldn't compete with such naturally

dangerous storms

and nature is the womb from where I was born.

Tempestuous in nature, I am a storm

but I wish you did not let me win.

//

I will jump over the cliff

and into the ocean

and I will let the waves swallow me up

and when my body has been ripped apart,

maybe then you will find a piece of me that you love.

//

You smiled at me

You smiled at me

and in your smiling

you saved my life.

Your eyes were kind

your face looked gentle

so I stepped off the ledge

because you smiled at me

and then you left

and I was back on it.

How weak

my spirit

how weak

when it feels it's forever lost

its most basic need.

//

I tried to fill the empty spaces inside of me

with little pieces of you

your words, your laughter...

I wanted to be whole

I wanted to feel complete

I thought that in finding you, I would find myself too

but little did I realize that

my soul can never be shared in the way my body can.

I lost track of my own feelings feeling you

and that is how I got lost

because the little pieces that were left of me

were then forever lost in you

because all I did was disarrange my pieces

to rearrange yours.

//

She was starving for love

she was craving its slap

she didn't want to give up

on finding love;

finding

searching

looking

pursuing

restless

frantic

angry

sadness

lonely

and famished for the opposite of everything she was

feeling

yet feelings are the key to bring life's gifts in.

//

She didn't know what made her happy

and that made her sad.

She didn't find in herself some company

and her company didn't want to hang out with the sad

which then made her sadder

and she knew she was just making herself sad

which made her saddest.

//

Nairobi is such a noisy city

both within the city

and inside the people in it.

//

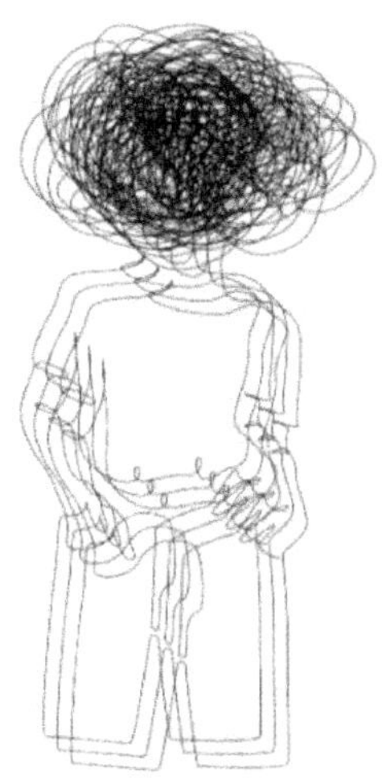

Never have I ever seen a generation so blue, depressed

and distraught

and yet so stupidly happy in a picture.

Never have I ever see struggle so perfectly clothed in

diamonds

while mining coal in their minds.

Never have I ever believed in the bigger picture

until I saw the damage of sadness that is currently with

us.

//

My heart was fizzing with a funny feeling

and I knew you would be the one to kill it.

Nonetheless, I let you be the camouflaged healer

I loved you, so I let you be the killer.

//

I wish it was safe for you to be yourself

for you to speak your truth

and not be afraid.

I pray we get there soon

too many lives get lost

hiding -afraid-

I wish the war on your end

finds some rest

and love find in your heart a nest.

I wish the world will soon

accept the weird bunch of the group.

Too many lives get lost

fearing expression of their self, and caught in that loop.

//

Her heart is beautiful but gluey

like thick honey that drips from a spoon

glistening gold, clingy with its hold.

//

We should have been taught how to knit ourselves a

net with which we can catch ourselves when we're

drowning in heartache or self-hate.

Now look at how many hearts and minds are breaking

in silence like a virus upsetting the balance of the

health of humanity.

Now its fatality upon fatality, evidence of the brutality

with which we have hammered down the core values

of humanity.

We should have been clothed in wool instead of

leather,

so we can remain humble and soft no matter the

weather.

We should have.

We can now.

//

The sky wheeze like an asthmatic kid

birds chirp like they've seen God

his cologne impregnates her nose

but love is not what she thought it was.

There is a God to worship on Sundays

a job to get to on Mondays.

The loud cling of responsibility chimes,

how can it be serene outside

but so chaotic inside?

//

I'll take down my Armor

and open myself up to love's wounds

craving that razor-sharp type of soul

that cuts through mine.

I'll let you bruise me

I'll let you use me.

I took down my amour

and opened myself up to love's wounds

craving the drama

that would cut through my many moods.

I let you use me

I let you bruise me

now look at bruised me

playing absentee in prose

from the responsibility

of taking care of me. //

What will be my succor for pain?

The paradox of co-existing anguish and happiness?

Flashes of humor in anger?

Nostalgic moments in between wine sips?

Or peace of mind in the acceptance of duality?

This range of human emotions,

dictates the future of a soon to be forgotten corpse.

I will kiss fear with this range

because I need to stop fearing change.

//

I need someone

that understands my pain

even before I feel it

someone that sees

the hurt in my eyes

even when I try to smile it away

someone who knows

when I need my space

before I even realize it.

That is the kind of someone I need

That is the kind of someone I miss.

//

Youth and I were once mates

as swans in love are swan mates.

We went on many a dates

and danced silly by silver gates.

Was I vain?

Did I over-romanticize beauty?

Was I the fool

or youth the romanticized thief?

A void began a blossoming

when further I approached my homecoming,

a void so far away from its home,

when my esthetics also began to roam.

//

The moon is lit up by 6 pm

-Full, like the life I dream of-

but I miss the crescent moon

weirdly shaped like me

not living up to its full potential

like me

at least that way I relate

relate to something half as good

something half as good like me.

//

Could it be that you inspired me

to write the saddest song ever?

Could it be that all the while

we wasted time together?

Could it be that this is it?

That this is how our story is?

That all we were

were sad pieces of hearts blown in to bits?

//

Poetry is a war waged for lovers and tragedy because

tragic horrors and broken hearts give birth to the best

poetry

not in the poem being tragically horrific

but in the development of mind and spirit because of

the tragically horrific.

"Write me a poem?"

"You're speaking my language.

Heck, I just might marry you for the damage."

//

Lying in bed

I stretch my arms out

towards the gaping space

in to the realm of doubt

a world of lying tongues

and deceitful eyes to boot.

Love-is-lost in this world

the love I lost is so lost

but was it love, this world of multiple tongues?

Was it love at all?

//

You feel hate

you feel anger

you feel lust

you feel love

towards your friend

towards your brother

towards your lover

towards your father

and you ask

and you cry

and you prevaricate

and you lie

about last night

about your last fight

about Fred and Mike

about your life.

//

I can't hold on to pretty little things

their prettiness is deceiving me

I'm trying not to look into the eye of fire

like a moth to a flame, unable to resist what it desires.

My legs have wandered to your cigarette

you have me captured like fish fruitlessly resisting a

net.

You have so many beautiful words which you say to me

and maybe this cigarette can repeat them to me.

You have so many secret worlds which you hide from

me

and maybe this cigarette can reveal them to me

it has been where your mouth has been

and that's much further than I have ever been.

But that's okay with me right?

Because I don't want to hold on to pretty things?

Because I'm trying to not fall for the flame's deceiving?

Right? Right? It's just a flaming cigarette and I'm a

moth that's sensed the heat

and I want to feel the heat of things,

things that friendship only cannot bring,

things that will force us to flap our wings,

and cling to the flame that our love could bring

If only I didn't desire you also in my dreams,

if only this dream was more than just a dream,

I would wake up tomorrow happy and beaming

if only I had you in my life with me.

//

21st century kids are drowning in an orgasm of

depression

but apparently, they like to swim

apparently, we like to swim

apparently, I'm a swimming athlete.

//

His hair is nothing special

it's just a plain bun

it's gloomy this twisted plot

of souls come undone.

Bacchus has come wet

with hemlock in span

to make me forget

'bout souls come undone.

'Tis the devil that made me

dirtify my nails

for a two-faced man

wherein all charm lies.

Till this day I cry

for thine muesli

as slowly I die

eating love's garbage profusely.

//

He whispered to me about unfathomable passion

like that of the water when it clings on to the barks of

trees

during a vast tsunami with the help of flooding.

I was foolish and silly

unrefined like a hillbilly

I was girl

who trusted his every word.

I'll pick a rose for you, beloved

and if I prick a finger or two

only you, my blood will spell.

Chapter in, chapter out

a story was born

one I thought I'd never mourn

but all stories have an end.

Love's lost, lust lasts forever

and gone is my stupid friend

with his stupid words

and my stupid heart.

//

I just want somebody to hold

somebody to touch.

I just want somebody to kiss

somebody to love

maybe somebody to flirt

or somebody to break my heart

I just want somebody.

//

I love that you love me

though you do not see me

your eyes are blind to my heart

your heart blind to my sins

and yet,

still, you love me

with a soul that can be called doom,

and a mind tainted by gloom,

you see stars in my eyes,

eyes that only sparkle for despair

if they sparkle at all

but still my love

you persist on this quest

that you do not call a quest at all

and love me still,

still, you love me.

//

192

He reveres her from afar

God's masterpiece come to life

dancing in the light

you enviable light.

Who can touch the whole of her?

He dares not approach

for he'd never want to disturb the -carefree,

(spine-bending, book-reading)- attention,

of a maiden fair as she.

Heavy is his heart for her love

his limerence dooms him

because of unrequited love.

//

I don't hurt because of you

I hurt because of the pain

that was caused by you

I try to get it out of me

because I don't want it eating me

I don't want the memories in my head

I don't want the scrambled feelings in my heart

I don't want the feel of you in my veins

You're the only poisoned blood burning me hot with

pain.

//

I swear if there is a hell after earth

then I will just have to die there too

because I can't do this alive thing twice

where suffering is the key to making you wise.

If heaven is real

and I find myself in it

then praise be

because suffering is not in heaven's musical keys

like it is in the rhythm of life.

//

If I showed you what is burning in my heart

you would melt away like wax

at the mere crack of first light.

You wouldn't know where to start

with scrapping off the blacks in the cracks

which will have no escape from the light.

//

They say what goes around

comes back around.

What is it that I did,

when I was in my mother's womb,

that planted the roots of my life in a tomb?

That made me deserve life's choking fumes?

Was I that dreadful of a fetus?

Did I make my mother throw up too violently?

Did I make her want to die?

Did I scratch her furiously from the inside,

or was my very existence karma in itself,

that all I want is to kill my life?

//

Sometimes a wolf wanders off to a farm

not hunting for a sheep or two to devour

but searching for something more than a great meal

something like the love he sees given to the sheep by

the shepherd.

He wonders what it would be like to be loved like that

what it would be like to have some company

how wool would feel like on his skin.

Sometimes he wonders and wanders

but always and always he is chased away.

It's a complement really, "we're scared of you,"

but even a wolf can crave some company too.

//

There is a void in each one of us that we constantly try to fill using sex, drugs, arguments, work, clubbing, obsession, desire for rejection (it's a thing), pornography, masturbation, the elation of cheating or sneaking around, etc. This list includes some pretty gnarly things as well but no one vice is greater than the other. Coveting and murder will both take you to hell: sin is sin.

Voids need to be filled because a hollow being begets an idle being and idleness is a major ingredient to evilness.

It's the kind of furnishing you use to fill that empty space that either pleases the mind or disturbs it but all in all; make peace with your pleasures and sins. They are crucial ingredients to what your life will be. Also, it's the only way to get over them if you're feeling guilty about it. You don't have to shout about weird cravings. Crave them silently but don't run away from them if they have refused to leave you.

The more you resist, the more you are drawn back to the urge. The more you accept, the less it feels like a task, the less it feels like it's a must then soon, it will disappear just like that or, hopefully, you will find a better replacement for it. Embrace yourself with all your black just as you have your white parts.

All I have is the love I offer

I hope that's enough

to quench your heart.

You see, I've always been a loner

and when I wasn't

I was the dull, ugly, fat friend

and I tried so hard to be my own friend

and when that happened

I found an abundance of love within myself.

I place it at your feet

Do what you will with it.

Yes, yes,

how can I give away such love like this?

What else is there but love

and lovers in disbelief?

I place it at your feet my love. //

It starts from the dry leaves

wilted grass

rot wood

tree's barks

the colored flowers

butterflies are next

bees, as tough as they are

are still caught in the horror.

The worms of the earth

they have it worse;

one by one

every living and dead thing

disintegrates

and it doesn't stop spreading.

It rages

it's wild and angry

and we try to quench its thirst

but fire has never made

love to grass silently

nor wood or anything it

touches .

In case you don't know

your love is this fire

and I'm the embodiment of vulnerability

dry as grass ready to turn crisp.

//

Bernard: Halt! Move no further, plunge no deeper.

Claris: Just a stranger you are. My ears bear not your warning.

Bernard: 'Tis common that man seeks to bend himself towards the grip of the afterlife but why so for a maiden fair as thee?

Claris: 'Tis with a heavy heart that I proceed.

Bernard: My good Lord! You're far too beautiful to end like this.

Claris: Season your admiration. The blessings of Aphrodite forsake me so and push me to my end.

Bernard: I want to pull at the joy strings of your heart. Please do not jump

Claris: Your certainty that overwhelms.

Bernard: I am but a man of my word.

A hop and a song and a baby was born. Six winters in,
Claris heard the nymphs deep down in the stream
calling to hop and to sing with them too.

'Tis with a *heavy* heart that she proceeded.

//

You gave me pixie dust,
and I wished for your heart.
I gave you my heart
and you gave me dust.

It's a dreadful world that we live in

so many broken souls just trying to fit in.

It's horrid what we have become

and we can't change the things we have already done.

//

It's such a shame

that all a heart as beautiful as hers wanted to do was

stop

Life felt like a game

that constantly demanded her to drop and hop and

never stop.

//

Our now will soon be past

and because we put lust first,

we will not last,

because we have put love last.

//

It was raining for a long while

so I looked for shelter.

I hid under a tree

against every advice.

The skies were angry

but they were also sad

so I let them be.

Even when lightning stroke down the tree,

I was afraid to move a muscle

too afraid to walk alone on a rainy day

for isn't that what lovers should do together?

And so I stayed a while longer

until the lightning stroke me down too.

//

You were the storm

but also the warm.

You were the lightning

and you struck every inch of me

that's why till this day

I have breathing difficulties.

//

You bottle up emotions

only to end up opening a bottle of pills

to help you feel again.

You avoid talking about your feelings

only to end up on a therapist's couch

crying your heart out.

You avoid going out with your friends

only to end up stalking them

when they appear on your social feed.

Who? Who? Who does any of this help?

//

Eyes closed and you could feel her skin against yours

Eyes closed and you could smell her lilac scent

Eyes closed and she was yours

Eyes closed and she was yours

but you had to open your eyes sometime.

//

I am here right now

I am alive

I exist

I am flesh and bone

I am breathing

My heart is beating

I am alive

-    Sometimes, a reminder is necessary

//

Sometimes

it's the devil that makes you smile the most:

the things he tells you that no one else knows

those secrets you hold so close

those mischievous ways of yours

all ignited by his single word

even when he's standing from afar.

You see,

the devil was not made to be ugly

though his ways be

so if he comes around, I promise he's going to be
charming

because that's just what he needs to bring out sin

and we fall for charms so easily as human beings.

//

How ironic is it

that some people

crave the feeling of life

so badly

that they try to die

to go look for it in another life?

//

She was loved

She had grace

She was pure of heart

and had a brave face.

She had everything but will

for her next breath.

She was pure with lust for death.

//

I am afraid

afraid that my love is too fierce

afraid that my love will consume your love

and you will be left with none

so I keep it to myself just in case.

As it goes, I'm too afraid to love

incase my love breaks your heart.

//

You thought chaos was beautiful

so you gave yourself

to all the wrong people as usual.

They took your love

and left you with the disarray

that continues to lead you astray.

Still,

if I asked you to walk towards me

and litter your path with thorns of false connections

you would fall for the misdirection of chaotic affection

over and over again.

-masochist

//

I felt a warmth on my cheek

and knew that summer was here

but as it goes

it passes

and much too soon did winter fall

and winter stayed.

I longed for a taste

of that summertime ray

but the cold

was much too stubborn

it literally

took my breath away;

you, literally

took my breath away.

Now I'm heaving with heartbreak.//

He dreams of being in a rock band

of traveling the world

of cooking for Madonna

of diving into the deepest parts of the ocean

of making love to a princess

and buying a beat up Chevrolet

and driving his son around town in it.

Then, he wakes up

cold and afraid

about the life he is living

and questions

his exponential potential.

Is he being brave ?

Is he playing into fate

or preparing his own plate? //

I want to tell you a story

about how I admire death.

It takes what it pleases, with such self-justification and

mockery

crude and diabolical as it may be

picking and deciding

whom it wishes to savor

at any moment of its choosing

and who is just too tasteless

to dance with it in the eternal flames.

I remember, more times than five,

I tried to gift my life to death

and give it more death in its life

using only but a kitchen knife.

Surprisingly so, he gave me back my life.

On a second attempt

taking up a sharp razor to my wrist

I once again did him tempt

but he refused, this gruesome beast.

Angry and disappointed

I went for the rope that cut before I could hang

then for the gun to my head I pointed

an empty magazine, a useless gun.

I started questioning this gruesome beast

late at night, with my shadow and I

but still it did not crack

assuring me; it'd be long

before I see the inside of a hearse.

XXI
THE WORLD

I guess I'm just too tasteless

too plain, too boring

even for the art of dying

especially for dear old death and his unfair timing.

What is fair is what I say is

but right now, I wish death could come lay with me.

//

I should tell you to run

to run away

from the darkness that surrounds *me*

the darkness that's inside of *me*

but I am selfish

and I want you here

I want you to choose *me*

I want you close to *me*

I want you to love *me*

and all that makes *me, me*

I want to be selfish with you

Selfish, I know.

//

'Tis like a dream within a dream

a portiere that lorgnette can't peer

yet I dream and dream again

of Gethsemane.

Like a flower that hides in dawn

you hid your petals from man's sight

for vanity was your portion

and so shall you die.

I was trekking to Calvary

eyes wide with internal blinds and scratch by my side

you took me to the promised land

premeditated.

With the strains of a wimpling voice

I sang of my hearts love to you

and you spoke with a knife-edged voice like a spitting
sky

saying, "I don't love you."

He calls me the Queen of duplicity

because all he does is run his mouth and all I do is sit

still and look pretty.

//

Satan smiled and stretched out his hand, I held on

saying "well here comes trouble now."

Satan was a troubled man and I was his girl.

Satan left me curled and shrunk

but isn't that what Satan does?

How couldn't I not have predicted that?

I suppose I loved you that bad.

//

Grief is just love with no place to go

no hand to hold

no skin, just stone.

I am deep

inside grief

and I can't swim.

Grief is just love that feels like it's lost its home.

//

I don't know what you see

when you look at me

when your blue eyes

come into contact with mine.

Do you notice the pain in my smile

or is my poker face a winner?

Do you swear you've never seen beauty

like the beauty you think is mine?

Whatever you think you see

please, unsee it

for all I can promise you from me

is a journey where true love can never be

because I do not know the true me

yet.

//

Because you are loved by me

you will hear my song

you will listen to my voice

and dance to the sound of my heartbeat

but my heart beats no more

and my voice's only a memory

my song a reminder

of the life I live no more.

//

The more I write,
the better I feel
but the sadder I get.
I don't know if writing
is healing or killing me
but I struggle with it
because it is me.

//

How I love to be loved

I love the word love

the way my tongue kisses my upper jaw

whenever I pronounce it.

Love, love, love,

you cannot stop it

but you can hide away from it

and sadly I do without a clue why this is true

but oh how I love love

and loves that love me.

//

For crumbs of your love
I'd gladly be the casualty.
That's what love does to me.

Now see if you can stomach
all my vanity
and all the dark you'd thought you'd never see

See if you can stomach banality
you with your wild wants and needs.
See if you can fathom it!

//

Don't fall for the pretending of things

When they go wrong, it's not what it seems

Don't shrivel your throat with silent screams

Silence is enlightening but sometimes it dims

I am learning to fall

and what it means to fly

I am learning to let go

of what doesn't want to be mine

I am kissing myself

In a calm breeze

I am finally able

to anticipate my most intimate needs

Xoxo,

Kendi.

Acknowledgement

To my beautiful mother for being my biggest supporter and allowing me space to make excuses for me to write. I love you and you deserve a world full of love. Mitchelle Makena, you have become one of my closest friends and as my sister, I thank God that we are friends too. I love you dear family for being there for me throughout this journey, and to my father for being absent for it.

Eric, your impact in my life is beyond explanation in words. Thank you for all you have been, for all you have given and continue to give.

All The Petals of the Universe *(preview)*

An undisputed rock solid paradise

This is the entry into the woodlands

An undisputed rock solid paradise

A heaven on earth covered with pasture

That you must develop, but first capture.

This is the space to set up shop

Karibu to the center of greenery in vast

A land of plenty, the shopping never stops

But if a black man drops dead, well, it's just a corpse!

The miners are always digging for gold

And suits biding in oil price wars

This is the place to steal the crop

And starve the farmer and auction his lot

And test for science the extent of disease

Then take the cure overseas.

White people are an authority Africans have come to trust

Clinging to the glow of promises vast

That once we dig and harvest our land

They'll turn our sand in to grass.

This is the place famine is ablaze

Just ask the white man with a cross on his face

Who then suits up and gets on a plane

And flies to Africa to make some change.

Come to Egypt and take pictures with the pyramids

And more photos –why not?- of bounties caught

And mount the trophies that you caught in the arid

At least you saved the rhino from draught.

Come to Africa, it is a land of plenty

And the price of living is not too hefty

And Africans, as you know, are as dumb as their cattle

Bottle the cheap labor and threaten them with battle

Ample are the songs sung by worried hearts

Passed from child to child about the past

The white man joins the camps and sparks further the fire

And passion engulfs the throats, the man is an amplifier!

Pride fills this man around the camp fire

That his presence demands the best of attire

And the Africans sing in their vernacular

The songs their forefathers wrote

Of surviving the white man's rip of their jugular.

Poem

You don't know why you look for crumbs
Why you pick so often at your scabs
Why you think the feast others eat
Is not part of your own feast.
Why do you doubt the wind
When it tries to push your wings?
You don't know why you can't just love
Without feeling an emotional flood.
All the colors you've ever know
Are fading away so subliminally
And you don't know what you did wrong
To go from fertile to barren land so quickly.
You and the hill you're ever climbing
You and the prayer in your chest bubbling
You don't know why you keep on waiting
To survive a tragedy that's not happening.
Oversized clothes make you feel secure
Is that why you want your parachute
To land in the middle of nowhere?
Hope in you is pale and without flowers
(Heaven is a place you desire to believe)
Heaven is real but you're not a follower
Every day you feel lower and lower.
Your heart's not fresh from healing
Just stabbing and repeating
You want this poem to reach its ending
You need this poem to do some mending
Blurry you, reading Virginia Wolf
Soft light from outside loving you
You feel as deeply as the ocean

Yet you are no boat
You cry more furiously than the rain
But you are not the storm.
Stars align the inside of your brain
You are a miracle, with just a few glitches
But you Virginia reading you
Poetry writing you
Always fighting you,
You fear there's no miracle in you.
A passport full of stamps in the wrong turn
Lies beside your bed with you
You fear you love the burn of the sun
And that is why you fry your heart.
Someone special has marked your heart for love
To blindfold your feelings in a lovely trap
You are leaking with vulnerability
And yet still you're seeking it
All metaphors can go to hell
This poem needs to end
You want so badly to be well
And the poem badly craves an ending
But this is the birth of art
Exiting the fence of a mind that needs mending
The ocean loves your droplets
Don't stay hidden too long in your closet
Love will always reveal to you
The colors which you try to hide
Love will always be to you
What you eventually decide
You poem loving, word-hugging you
Love is always by your side

And if you are feeling otherwise
LOVE IS BY YOUR SIDE.
What your hands did do was hold you
And that is what your heart didn't do
Inside it felt deserted to you.
Your favorite person is not you
And that's a nightmare you never thought would come
true.
All you sing is love songs
With breasts out your chest
You were taught how to love wrong
Before you outgrew your mother's nest
And now the nightmare is in your chest
In your head, your chest, your head, your chest.
Soft
Supple
Sun
You are loved
Heal my love
You are loved.
You almost bloom
But you must write what you must write
You think no light is governing you
Yet you don't lack the words to write
Harmonize the keys in your black and white
If you want music, play every beat you like
You who know better
Than to walk in a rainy day,
Walk in a rainy day.
Vividly dream and jump with both feet
Into the paint that colors joy

You don't know why the divine feels like it's missing
Like it's kissing everyone else
Except you who need the kissing
Here you are, full of breath
Beguiling with your beauty
So overwhelmed by the darkness
That came to emphasize your shining
Nothing is late
I hope you'll be able to relate
Drink the wine of poetry
If it neutralizes your suffering
You are the depth you are looking for,
The heart you search for with your heart.
You are more than a hand will ever hold
You need to let the latent go
Fragments of friction attack outer you
Life's miniscule debris seems flattering
Fragments of friction attack inner you
You flirt with miniscule debris
Pause
See that you are not remotely close to your magic
Then see yourself have it.
You're punished with rejection
Is what you think
You want to break free from that deception
Because it's what's making you sink
Why do you doubt the great height
To which your wings have the right?
You don't know why you just can't love
When love tries to push your wings.
You eyes shutting, sleep wanting you

4 am sleeping you
Don't deny you're overflowing,
Tickled and tackled by your aching dreams
You do not want to fall into false dreams
With false hope of blooming
5 am sleeping you
The night came running for you
Too late did you refuse its call
If you were even to refuse at all
The light was meant to catch you
Even if it was late
The sky was meant to fly you
And aid your ascend to the moon
No lie was meant to find you
But so so many did mark you
You want to heal your feelings
But dry eyes abandon you
An explosion looks like you?
We'll that's just not true.
The flutter of wings
Didn't always scare you
The reason the view's not there is because
To see both the forest and the ocean
You first have to let yourself fly
And whether you float or die
You will not find the answer
While lying on your back.
Only after the jump.
You wring the water out of words
And splash in the puddles you create

You dread what you're running towards
But at least you create

You are who you choose to become
And you are not small at all
Get up from that floor
You word-hugging you!

Ps: I am done.
        -poem

Frayed nerves

I won't correct that I'm the girl you used to know
Because since we last met
I took a bite off the ripeness of rage redefined
And as it slid down my throbbing throat
I clutched at the vines of defiance
And held myself up with the thought
That all men are liars

I won't correct that last we met my bells were set
Because you will ask where the ring went
I count my luck for the invention of gloves
And a mind that can lie well
I won't tell you the ring's a trophy
And neither say the man that took it
Took much more than all rings value that are deemed
worthy

I won't correct that I'm better now because my figure
is slimmer
Because before we last met
My drawers were not teeming with pills
And I was on no health regime
I drink my food like a snowflake melts in the heat
And remember the path that led me
To believe all men are liars

No fruit can my kindled fire birth
Or Broom broom enough to sweep all the dirt
Of that day's struggle to escape his catch

But catch he did and pinned me to the earth
It's frightening how frayed nerves can leave one red
How certain types of dirt can never shed
Even when you wash yourself with the bleach that
washes the dead

No great story ever started with the truth
Or that man in grey would not have had his way
Of bittersweet takes I've got the bitter
But when with him, I thought I had the sweet
It's only when I strangled the grass, I knew
How much bad a good face could hide - and man be
crass,
Even when it's breaking glass between my thighs

Nest your questions in another's bed
Only ask me about the day ahead
Once upon a time, a man I knew
Became a beast with an infectious disease
Invited me out for a drink, and
Hinged my dreams with the accompaniment of
screams
Eventually I learnt, people are not what they seem

I won't correct that I'm the girl you used to know
I won't correct that last we met my bells were set
I won't correct that I'm better now because my figure
is slimmer
I won't reveal how no fire can rekindle my dangling
fruits
Or how bitter the taste between my legs

Or how I scream ceaselessly in bed
Because you're right
I'm doing fine. And you?

Yours is the kingdom of heaven on earth

When you are tied to the chasing of pleasure,
You are tied to the experience of pain.
For what is pleasurable is fleeting,
And that which leaves breaks our hearts.

When that pleasure you seek resides within
What you seek without seems undoubtedly
demeaning,
For wherever you go, so shall it be,
And you shall call it Joy,
And you, shall enjoy!

When there is darkness from north to south,
And you can see the glint from the reflection of your
eyes,
Standing by the window, in the deserted night,
And you can be taken in by this boring delight,
Yours is heaven, and you are experiencing it.

When nothing externally grand could add to the
multiverse of your dancing reflection,
nor loss too tragic as to make you decide life is not
worth the debris it scatters,
And when with your loss you pick the glass with
bloodied hands,
Tell not a soul and carry on Piecing the Puzzle of life
back together,
As if you had planned this greater loss
And were simply playing a part in a forgotten play,

And you go about your way and make merry anyway,
Yours is the kingdom of heaven on earth.

POETRY BOOKS BY THIS AUTHOR

All The Petals Of The Universe 1 & 2

The Cages We Built

What I Mean When I Talk About Love

Liquid Love

Knitting My Soul

Fiction books

Seduced By A Virgin

Life in No Order: A Compilation of Short Stories

Self help

The Six-figure Lifestyle: 42 Small Changes That Will

Make You a Millionaire

Knitting
my
Soul
KENDI KARIMI

WHAT I MEAN
WHEN I TALK ABOUT
LOVE
KENDI KARIMI

LIQUID
LOVE
KENDI KARIMI

ALL
THE
PETALS
OF
THE
UNIVERSE
KENDI KARIMI KENDI KARIMI KEND

ALL
THE
PETALS
OF
THE
UNIVERSE 2
KENDI KARIMI KENDI KARIMI KEND

KENDI KARIMI
THE
CAGES
WE
BUILT
OF PASSION AND DEPRESSION
a moving and deeply felt collection

KENDI KARIMI
IFE
IN NO O
R
D
E
R

KENDI KARIMI
SEDUCED BY A
VIRGIN

THE SIX-FIGURE
LIFESTYLE
42 SMALL CHANGES
THAT WILL MAKE YOU
A MILLIONAIRE
BY KENDI KARIMI

Seduced By A Virgin

Rude girls, church boys, desire honey eyes and guns.

What could go wrong? Let's
add some spice with a sprinkle
of romance. Or maybe a
handful. Heck, let's squeeze the
juice out of love!

I know what you want, but I can't give it.

Life In No Order: A compilation of short stories

A head scratching, heart stopping collection of stories.

Stories are never just stories
the same way love isn't just
love or hate just hate. With
love, you make the life-
altering decision to live and
die by your lover's side when

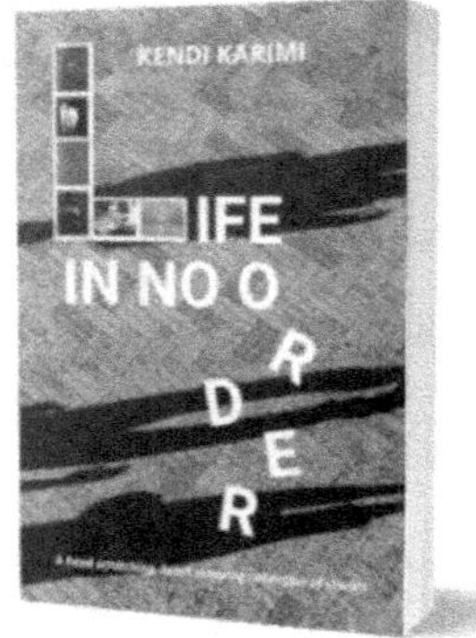

marriage come along. With hate, you bully a child into submission, into self-loathing, into depression.

With stories, you tell about your share of pain and joy, love and hate and in doing so, you knit a lovely invisible creation that sheds light on culture and history as is in your time. You have the chance to immortalize something with a story, a chance to shine the torch on life.

Life in no order is a collection of short stories that talk about life, in no order.

About the author

Kendi Karimi is a professional journalist with rich

experience in

writing. She

graduated top of

her class with

first-class honors

in Mass

Communication.

She has worked in and written for media houses,

newspapers, blogs, magazines, and creative institutions

and is currently a full-time writer.

Her short story, 'What Does It Mean To Be Kind

Anyway' was shortlisted for the Wakini Kuria prize for

children's literature. Kendi has also been awarded a

certificate of recognition by BIC group and participated

in various international anthologies. She is a poet who

writes about love and life in a tragically beautiful

manner, and adds a poeticism deeply rooted in

philosophy and well-being to her stories.

She is also an artist who enjoys the occasional play with

canvas and music composition. Curious? Watch her

music video 'Let You Go' on youtube. Kendi hopes to

become a fully-fledged creative entrepreneur and live a

life of open expression through her art.

I'm a poet for the lovers, dreamers and believers. For

the hope give-ups and the heart beat ups. If you live to

read rhyme, you will love the lines in mine.

Happiness lies in the balance of how you perceive the world around you and the measurement of your expectations. Only I, as only you, can fully know the degree of your own suffering and only we, individually, can encourage the cycle or break it.

9 789914 707182